QUANTUM READER

Read Fast, Comprehend More, Move On

Bobbi DePorter

Welcome to the
Quantum Upgrade Book Series

Reading helps you discover your passions, follow your interests, and get what you want out of life. It's where smarts get their start – your reason for genius! When quantum readers want to know something, they find the answers instead of letting the idea slip away. To do this, you not only need reading skills to keep up with your curiosity; you need a powerful reading system to apply your skills to learning more about the things that matter to you. This book provides a six-step system to read faster, comprehend more, and find the ideas that will spark your potential.

In today's quantum world, you need fast skills and vast knowledge to learn more, be more and do more. Use your reading upgrade to expand your ideas and get the results you want out of school and life.

The Quantum Upgrade Book Series:

Quantum Learner
Quantum Reader
Quantum Writer
Quantum Memorizer
Quantum Thinker
Quantum Note-Taker

QUANTUM READER

Read Fast, Comprehend More, Move On

LEARNING FORUM PUBLICATIONS

Published by Learning Forum Publications

Copyright © 2007 by Bobbi DePorter

Submit all requests for reprinting to:

Learning Forum Publications
1938 Avenida del Oro
Oceanside, CA 92056
(760) 722-0072

Cover and interior design: Stephen Schildbach
Illustrations: Jonathan Fischer
Book concept: John Pederson
Editor: Sue Baechler

Library of Congress Control Number: 2006940415

ISBN-10: 0-945525-42-7
ISBN-13: 978-0-945525-42-4

Printed in the United States of America

To the Quantum Learner who wants to learn more,
be more and do more in school and life.

Enjoy all six of our books:
Quantum Learner, Quantum Reader,
Quantum Writer, Quantum Memorizer,
Quantum Thinker and Quantum Note-Taker.

Contents

Read Fast, Comprehend More, Move On
Becoming a Quantum Reader

You already have reading skills that work – just not as well as they could. We all have our own reasons to upgrade our reading. For Albert Einstein, it was physics – for Bill Gates, a computing renaissance – and for JK Rowling, a storytelling dream. But before $E=mc^2$, Microsoft, or Harry Potter, there were multiplication tables to memorize, piles of articles to read, and rough drafts to write.

Any success, no matter how large or small, starts with reading, writing and memory. When we first learned these skills, they were fun and exciting. However, for many of us, reading turned into homework, writing became a chore, and memory triggered thoughts of multiple-choice exams.

Today, we read more – but not more effectively. With so many books to read and ideas to discover, it becomes more and more difficult to find the time to upgrade our reading skills. Yet we are living in a quantum world, where we need to be ready with fast skills and vast knowledge to learn more, be more and do more.
This book provides the skills and knowledge to upgrade your reading speed and comprehension. You will learn

a powerful six-step system to read faster and comprehend more – more of the things that matter to you.

*Before we get started, let's measure your current
reading speed.*

- Skip ahead to *The Einstein Factor* on page 49.

- Read the story for exactly one minute.

- Mark the last line you read and multiply the number
  of lines read by 8 to estimate your reading rate in
  words per minute.

  Write that number here: _____

- Answer the corresponding comprehension questions
  at the end of the story. Write your score below.

  _____ correct out of _____ questions

- Calculate your comprehension score by dividing the
  number of correct answers by the total number of
  questions answered. Multiply the answer by 100 and
  write your score below.

  Comprehension Score: _____

- Fill in the chart on the next page with your answers.

*When you're finished, return to Chapter 1 to start your
quantum reader upgrade.*

	BEFORE LEARNING THE QUANTUM READER SYSTEM	AFTER LEARNING THE QUANTUM READER SYSTEM
READING RATE Number of lines read in one minute × 8 (estimated number of words per minute)		
NUMBER OF QUESTIONS ANSWERED		
NUMBER OF CORRECT ANSWERS		
COMPREHENSION SCORE Correct÷Total × 100		

Chapter 1: Prepare

Get Ready to Read at Your Quantum Speed

Your upgrade is in progress

You can't simply tell your brain to read faster and comprehend more, but you can ask it to – so to speak. Asking the right questions before you read will spark your motivation and curiosity, preparing you to read at your quantum speed.

One of the most important questions to ask yourself is: *What's in it for me?* (or WIIFM for short, pronounced WHIFF-EM). WIIFM is the benefit we get from our actions, the question your brain asks itself, either consciously or subconsciously, to decide what it wants to remember. From the simplest daily tasks to monumental life-altering decisions, everything has to promise some degree of personal benefit, or you have no motivation to do it. Even the most selfless actions have a degree of WIIFM. For example, helping others gives you personal and moral satisfaction – that's what's in it for you! Sometimes the WIIFM is very clear in your mind, other times you have to look for it – or even invent it.

WIIFM is important because it can help you connect to your intrinsic motivation. This type of motivation is the most effective for learning because it's something you want to do for yourself, not for the teacher or your parents (that would be extrinsic motivation). Activities that are personally rewarding, interesting and joyful appeal to your intrinsic motivation. You do it because you want to. If you love your school or the work you do, you'll show up on time simply because you want to be there. If you're fascinated by a new computer program, you will learn it for fun and start using it

Quantum readers have instant access to their power switch: their intrinsic motivation.

to improve your performance. You do it because you enjoy it – it's that simple.

You can't be intrinsically motivated about everything you do, but searching for this type of motivation as often as possible will improve your end results – whatever the task.

Help your brain find the intrinsic motivation to become a quantum reader. Search for your intrinsic motivation!

QOOGLE | Intrinsic Motivation

Discover New Interests and Passions
Could've, would've, should've, DID IT!
Read more to do more of the things you love.

More Time with Friends
Go to a movie. Go shopping. Call your best friend. Spend time with the people who matter to you.

More Success
Get better grades. Earn more respect. Impress your friends and family.

Bookmark this page and return to it often. Keeping your motivation up to date and in the front of your mind is essential for upgrading your reading skills.

Motivating Both Sides of Your Brain

We primarily use the left hemisphere of our brain
when we read because it's geared for logical thought.
However, boosting your reading speed and comprehension means getting the right hemisphere involved
too. Right-brain activity is more holistic, rhythmic,
colorful and imaginative. Stimulating both sides
of your brain helps it work faster, harder and more
effectively. It's like putting on a play: You need orga-
nized planning and strategic fundraising, as well as
creative actors. Regardless of which role you're most
comfortable with, it's important to realize that we can
all increase our comprehension by creating pictures in
our minds of what we're reading. That's because our
brains create images to make meaning.

Ask Yourself Questions

Now that you have used WIIFM to find your intrinsic motivation, pique your curiosity with specific questions about what you're about to read. Ask yourself questions about the content like: *What's here that interests me? What does the author mean by this?* Your comprehension increases as your mind searches for the answers. The questions get you thinking about the material.

Prepare Your Reading Space

Get ready to apply your motivation and follow your curiosity by preparing your reading space. Do you have good lighting, a comfortable chair, a table to support your book, a highlighter, colored pens and paper for taking notes? Taking care of these details before you read will help you stay focused and reading at your top speed. Eliminate distractions by posting a note on your door while you're reading, or make an agreement with family members that gives you a chunk of time without disturbance.

Helpful tip: Decide how many pages or chapters you'll read before you start and mark your finish place. This improves your concentration because you are less likely to stop in the middle of your reading to see how much is left.

You've prepared your motivation, curiosity and reading space, now it's time to get into state.

Chapter 2:
Get Into State

Check Your Connection

Your upgrade is 20% complete

Have you ever finished reading a whole page or section of material and had no idea what you just read? That's because you weren't picturing the material in your mind. Your brain needs images to comprehend meaning; otherwise, you're just looking at text. But to picture the material and make meaning out of what you read, you need to be in the right state of mind: one of positive beliefs and focused concentration. Let's start with your beliefs.

Belief: Your Brain's Antivirus

Most of us don't understand how wireless Internet or text messages work. Nevertheless, we believe they will, and we use them to exchange important information.

To read fast and comprehend more, you must engage the same power of belief. You have to know that you can upgrade your reading. Positive beliefs will also help you find the intrinsic motivation you need to become a quantum reader.

Use the power of picturing to trash your old, negative ideas and frustrations about reading. This baggage motivated you to pick up this book – but that's as far as it's going to take you. Here's what to do:

- **Close your eyes and imagine that you are sitting at a computer.**

- **Open a blank word processing document.**

- **Make a list of all your bookish baggage like:** *I'm a slow reader. I hate reading. I get embarrassed when I have to read to others.*

- **Now save the document and give it a name like, Reading 1.0, I hate reading.com, or whatever fits the items on your list.**

- **Next, drag the document into the trash and empty the folder. Imagine your frustrations and bookish baggage being scrambled into trillions of digital fragments – out of your head and out of your life forever!**

You just trashed your frustrations with the power of picturing. Now fill the free space with positive beliefs.

Close your eyes, relax and let these thoughts sink into your subconscious mind. See yourself powering through homework assignments quickly and effortlessly. Imagine having time to read what you want or hang out more with your friends. Think of the time you will save as a quantum reader. How will you spend it? Filling your brain with these positive thoughts and beliefs will keep your bookish baggage in the trash and clear the way for upgraded concentration and commitment.

Boost Your Concentration:
Get into Alpha State

When you think about the word "concentration," what images come to mind? Whatever you pictured, it probably didn't look like this:

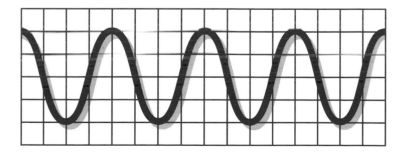

The image above represents an alpha brainwave. Scientists use a machine called an electroencephalograph (EEG) to measure and distinguish different states of brainwave activity. They have identified the alpha state as the most effective for learning.

Here's a rundown of the four main categories, or states, of brainwave activity:

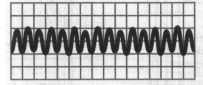

Beta—Awake, alert, and active. In beta, your brain is attending to many different stimuli at once. Activity is scattered. You may be thinking of many things at the same time or jumping from one activity to another. Four Instant Message conversations at once – that's your beta waves at work.

Alpha—A state of relaxed concentration. You're calm and alert, absorbing material and making connections. You are completely focused on one activity. It could be your favorite sitcom or a challenging game of chess. This is the best state for learning. Quantum readers ride alpha waves wherever they want to go.

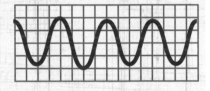

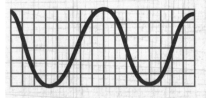

Theta—Your brainwaves are slowing down, just seconds away from a deep sleep. This is where you dream and process information.

Delta—The slowest brainwave state. You're in a deep sleep.

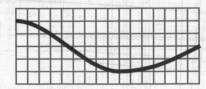

Most of us bounce between these different states without noticing it. But quantum readers have instant access to their alpha state – and so can you!

To get into alpha state, begin by creating a special place for your mind to go before you start reading. To create your special place, close your eyes, letting them roll up. This puts you in a visual state for learning. Now, picture a place where you feel relaxed and peaceful. It could be a favorite vacation spot or a special room at home. What does it look, smell and feel like? Picture yourself in this place as you begin relaxing. Do this for a few minutes to save your special place in your mind.

Now that you have your special place, let's try the whole process. Here's how:

Use your entire body. Your brain takes automatic cues from your body. If you're a sloucher, this can work against you because your brain interprets your posture as boredom. If you are lying down, your brain thinks it's time to sleep and releases chemicals that make you sleepy. Luckily, you can also use these cues to boost your concentration, and get into alpha state.

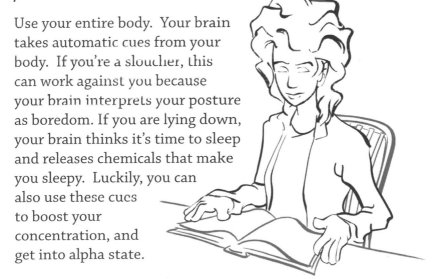

15

Sit up straight in your chair with both feet on the floor. Take a deep breath. Now close your eyes, roll them up, and picture your peaceful place. When you're ready, open your eyes and look down at your book. Practice this process until you can do it without thinking about each step. Remember to go through this exact sequence every time you're about to read.

Memorize this sequence and use it every time you want to read faster and comprehend more. It's a critical step to becoming a quantum reader.

Here's a rhyme to help you remember this critical skill:

- **Sit up straight in your chair.**

- **Take a deep breath of air.**

- **Close your eyes, roll 'em up, and find your peaceful spot.**

- **Open your eyes and read what you've got.**

Make a commitment:

Boosting your motivation, beliefs and concentration is not a one-time upgrade; it takes long-term commitment. If you're ready to believe in and work towards your success, take a moment to read the following agreement carefully. Sign and date it if you wish to proceed.

A NOT-SO-SERIOUS CONTRACT

I _____ [print your name here]
agree to believe in myself and my untapped
potential. I understand that – with my
commitment – this upgrade will improve my
reading speed and comprehension. I realize that
I am solely responsible for the resulting personal,
social and academic success. Furthermore, I am
prepared for the massive amounts of free time,
knowledge and personal benefit that I will enjoy
as a quantum reader.

_____   _____

Signature   date

Chapter 3: Use Eye and Hand Skills

Point, Click and Comprehend

```
████████░░░░░░░░░░░░
```

Your upgrade is 40% complete

Our brains want to read quickly. But we usually slow things down, thinking that if we read slowly, we'll understand the material better. In reality, this can have the opposite effect. Reading slowly can be boring. When we slow down, our minds wander and we miss information. Keep up with your curiosity and quantum brain with these eye and hand skills.

Upgrade Your Browser: Eye Skills

Most of us read one word at a time. But our minds can actually comprehend much more, especially when motivated and filled with positive belief. Words have greater meaning when we see them grouped together because they're in context. This takes peripheral vision.

Measure Your Peripheral Vision

Put your arms straight out in front of you with your hands in fists, thumbs up. Slowly move your hands out to each side, keeping your eyes straight ahead. Stop your arms just before your thumbs get out of view. Everything in sight and between your thumbs is part of your peripheral vision. Most people can see up to 45 degrees in each direction from straight ahead without moving their eyes. If this is true for you, the range of your peripheral vision is 90 degrees.

Here's another exercise: Look at the box on the next page. Focus your eyes on the letter "A" in the center of the alphabet and find which letter you can see without moving your eyes. Can you see out to "D", "G", or maybe even all the way out to "J"? As you become a quantum reader, your peripheral vision will improve. Return to this exercise later to measure your progress.

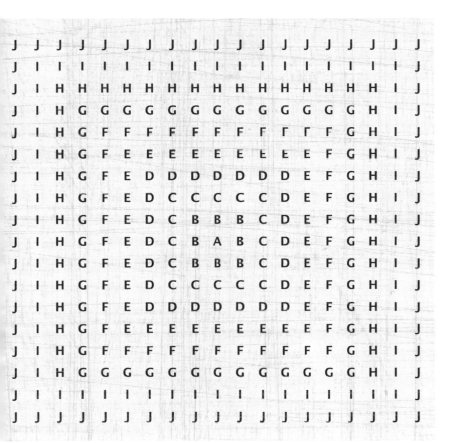

```
J  J  J  J  J  J  J  J  J  J  J  J  J  J  J  J  J  J  J
J  I  I  I  I  I  I  I  I  I  I  I  I  I  I  I  I  I  J
J  I  H  H  H  H  H  H  H  H  H  H  H  H  H  H  I  J
J  I  H  G  G  G  G  G  G  G  G  G  G  G  G  H  I  J
J  I  H  G  F  F  F  F  F  F  F  F  F  F  G  H  I  J
J  I  H  G  F  E  E  E  E  E  E  E  E  E  F  G  H  I  J
J  I  H  G  F  E  D  D  D  D  D  D  E  F  G  H  I  J
J  I  H  G  F  E  D  C  C  C  C  C  D  E  F  G  H  I  J
J  I  H  G  F  E  D  C  B  B  B  C  D  E  F  G  H  I  J
J  I  H  G  F  E  D  C  B  A  B  C  D  E  F  G  H  I  J
J  I  H  G  F  E  D  C  B  B  B  C  D  E  F  G  H  I  J
J  I  H  G  F  E  D  C  C  C  C  C  D  E  F  G  H  I  J
J  I  H  G  F  E  D  D  D  D  D  D  E  F  G  H  I  J
J  I  H  G  F  E  E  E  E  E  E  E  E  E  F  G  H  I  J
J  I  H  G  F  F  F  F  F  F  F  F  F  F  G  H  I  J
J  I  H  G  G  G  G  G  G  G  G  G  G  G  G  H  I  J
J  I  I  I  I  I  I  I  I  I  I  I  I  I  I  I  I  I  J
J  J  J  J  J  J  J  J  J  J  J  J  J  J  J  J  J  J  J
```

Focus

Have you ever tried to see a hidden image in a 3-D poster? If you have, you know that it helps to stare at the middle of the picture and relax your eyes. You can use similar focusing skills to read faster and comprehend more.

Soft Focus

Use "soft focus" to boost your reading stamina and speed. To activate your soft focus, follow the white space between lines of text rather than the letters. Your peripheral vision will see the line above. Soft focus increases your reading power by helping you absorb more text with less eye fatigue.

Tri-Focus

International trainer, consultant and quantum reader, Steve Snyder, can breeze through four books per night by using his tri-focus reading technique. His brain gobbles up 5,000 words per minute by visually dividing lines of type into thirds. This allows his eyes to read several words at once by jumping from group to group instead of from word to word. Practice this yourself with the tri-focus exercise below. Time yourself to see how much faster you read with this method, and compare it to your score from the first reading exercise. You can practice this method any time by closing your eyes and imagining a book in front of you. Move your eyes left, center and right repeatedly. Snap your fingers to the rhythm. Do this any time you have a few extra minutes between classes, while sitting in the doctor's waiting room or riding the bus.

"Tri" your focus with the following excerpt from QLN Magazine

Quantum learners	take ownership of	their personal and
academic success,	transforming what	many observers
refer to as the	"Trophy Kid	Generation."
According to	Stephen Mintz,	director of the
American Cultures	Program at Houston	University, many
of today's students	have become extensions	of their parents'
sense of self in	unprecedented ways.	According to his
book *Huck's Raft:*	*A History of American*	*Childhood* (2004),
"More and more of	their dawn-to-dusk	activities are
controlled by their	parents' sense of self	– not the child's
talents or interests."	But this is not true for	quantum learners
who have the reading,	writing, memory and	note-taking skills
to follow their	curiosities and discover	their passions.

(Read the full version of this article, Trophy Kids are Out, by requesting it from www.QLN.com.)

Both soft-focus and tri-focus exercises will help you group words together to read faster, but it's going to take some practice to break your old reading habits. This is why commitment counts.

The Need for Speed
Read faster – that's an order!

Air force pilots developed focusing techniques to identify enemy planes in combat. Eventually, researchers began refining and teaching these skills with great success. Realizing that the perceptual abilities of the eyes had been vastly underrated, the Air Force looked for new ways to apply their findings. They soon discovered that readers could comprehend up to four words flashed simultaneously on a screen for only one five-hundredth of a second!

Soon others adopted this approach, and eventually most speed-reading courses utilized the Air Force's focusing technique. For a while, most students enjoyed drastic increases in their reading speed. However, they reported a general dissatisfaction several weeks after the training because – when the course ended – their motivation dropped and so did their reading speed. Today, the same principle holds true for any speed-reading technique, so remember: Stay motivated and committed to boost your reading speed and become a quantum reader.

The Mystery of Mind Function, the Power of Soft Focus

The power of soft-focus reading techniques continues to impress those who try them out. You might have received the following popular email forward from a friend or family member:

> Cdnuolt blveiee taht I cluod aulaclty uestdnanrd waht I was rdanleg. The phaonmneal pweor of the hmuan mnid, aoccdrnig to a rscheearch at Cmabrigde Uinervtisy, it deosn't mttaer in waht oredr the ltteers in a wrod are, the olny iprmoatnt tihng is taht the frist and lsat ltteer be in the rghit pclae. The rset can be a taotl mses and you can sitll raed it wouthit a porbelm. Tihs is bcuseae the huamn mnid deos not raed ervey lteter by istlef, but the wrod as a wlohe. Amzanig huh? yaeh and I awlyas tghuhot slpeling was ipmorantt!

Drag and Drop: Hand Skills

When you first learned to read, you ran your finger along the words to keep your place. Later, you were told that this isn't the way "big people" read and that it slows you down. While it's true that most adults don't read with their fingers, it isn't because it slows them down. Studies show that using a visual guide, such as your finger or a pencil, actually speeds your reading by keeping you from backtracking.

See for yourself:

Sit face-to-face with a friend. Ask him or her to look about six inches above your head and move his eyes around your face in a circle. (He should only move his eyes – not his head.) You'll notice his eyes move in spurts and jerks – not in a smooth circle. Now, do it again, but this time ask your friend to use his finger to trace the circle. Notice how his eyes continuously move forward with the help of a visual guide.

Move your finger just below the text you're reading, keeping your eyes just ahead of your finger. As you come to the end of a line, quickly move to the line below. Push yourself to move a little faster than is comfortable. Use your peripheral vision to take in a third of a line at once.

Today, those numinous eyes, bushy mustache, and shock of silver hair remain the quintessential image of "genius," the name a synonym for supernormal intelligence. But as a child Albert Einstein appeared deficient. Dyslexia caused him difficulty in speech and reading.

You may stop and re-read words because you think you missed something, but if you're focused, you'll get it. You must keep moving forward to increase your reading speed. Your eyes will move faster and more efficiently when pushed along by your finger. We call this upgrade "the quick fix" because using a visual guide alone can double your reading speed.

27

Chapter 4: Superscan

Prime Your Mind

Your upgrade is 60% complete

I n most cases, combining reading and snowboarding or skiing would not be a good idea. But the halfpipe and skiing superscan skills described in this chapter are a perfect combination. Both skills are simple hand motions that prime your mind for reading.

Try them yourself:

Using your index finger, make a halfpipe "U" pattern spanning both pages. Or, use a back-and-forth pattern down the pages like a skier slaloming down the slope. These two superscan skills will help you get familiar with a lot of information in a short period of time. Have fun noticing interesting pictures, phrases or words while you're superscanning. Say to yourself, *What's that? Wow, neat picture. What's this about?*

These questions get your mind interested in what you're about to read.

Don't worry about reading specific words at this point – just practice the movements. You'll increase comprehension as you improve your peripheral vision.

Page turning might not be as exciting as skiing or snowboarding, but it is an additional hand skill that will help you maintain your momentum while superscanning.

This page-turning technique keeps quantum readers moving ahead without breaking their concentration. *(The directions on page 31 are for right-handed readers. Left-handed individuals should use the opposite hand of what's specified.)*

When you're ready, combine your page-turning technique and skiing or halfpipe by turning pages with your left hand as you scan with your right.

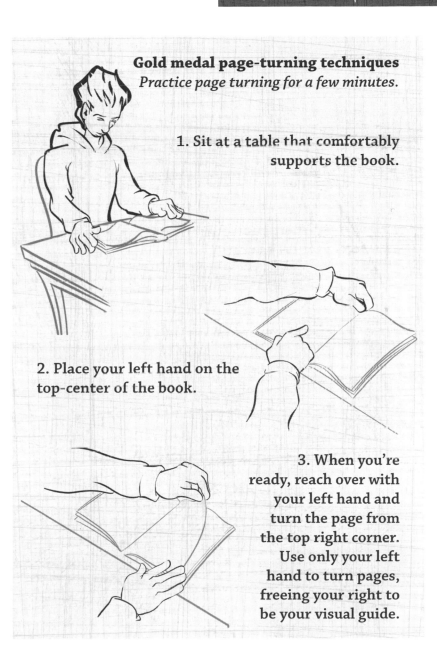

Gold medal page-turning techniques
Practice page turning for a few minutes.

1. Sit at a table that comfortably supports the book.

2. Place your left hand on the top-center of the book.

3. When you're ready, reach over with your left hand and turn the page from the top right corner. Use only your left hand to turn pages, freeing your right to be your visual guide.

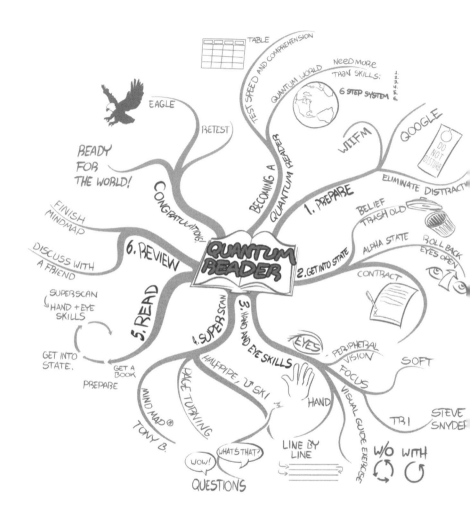

A MIND MAP OF THIS BOOK

After you're finished superscanning, make a **Mind Map®** of the material.

Making a Mind Map will help you organize and connect your ideas. Tony Buzan first developed this note-taking skill, which has been used by thousands of quantum readers to boost their reading comprehension. Here's how it works: First, write the title or main topic of your reading material in the middle of a new sheet of paper. You can circle it, make it bold or even create an image to make its meaning stand out. Draw thick lines from the center to create branches and write chapter headings or main ideas on the branches. Add new thoughts and relationships as they pop into your head on thinner lines at the end of each branch.

You'll find more Mind Mapping and other note-taking skills in *Quantum Note-Taker*.

You are now a superscanner – one step closer to becoming a quantum reader. You'll use this skill for your fastest reading or to preview material. Now that you have the superscanning skills to keep up with your upgraded motivation, beliefs and concentration, it's time to stop, put it together, and read.

Chapter 5: Read

Stop, Put It Together, and Read

Your upgrade is 80% complete

Locate a book or article that you want or need to read. Now, go through the steps again, this time putting them all together. Below are the first four steps of the quantum reader system. Step five is applying these steps to read something that matters to you.

1. Prepare
2. Get into State
3. Use Eye and Hand Skills
4. Superscan

1. Prepare

Find your intrinsic motivation with WIIFM. Ask yourself, "What's in it for me to read faster, comprehend more and learn this material?" Remember to activate as much of your brain as possible with both right and left-brain thinking. Use specific questions to pique your curiosity in what you're about to read. Ask yourself questions like: *What's here that interests me? What does the author mean by this?* Think of some possible answers. Remember, comprehension increases as your mind searches for the answers.

Get ready to apply your motivation and follow your curiosity by preparing your reading space. Do you have good lighting, a comfortable chair, a table to support your book, a highlighter, colored pens and paper for taking notes? Taking care of these details and eliminating distractions before you read will help you stay in an effective learning state and maintain your top reading speed.

2. Get Into State

Trash old frustrations and replace them with belief in your ability to become a quantum reader. Limit your distractions. When you're ready, prepare for focused concentration by getting into alpha state.

Remember to use this sequence every time you want instant access to alpha brainwaves – your most powerful learning state.

- **Sit up straight in your chair.**
- **Take a deep breath of air.**
- **Close your eyes, roll 'em up, and find your peaceful spot.**
- **Open your eyes and read what you've got.**

3. Use Eye and Hand Skills

Remind yourself to use soft focus and tri-focus to expand your peripheral vision and see groups of words at once. Place your left hand at the top of the book to turn the pages, and use your right index finger as a guide. Move your finger just below the text you're reading, keeping your eyes just ahead of your finger. Remember to move a little faster than is comfortable, and use your peripheral vision to take in a third of a line at once.

4. Superscan

Use the halfpipe and ski skills to scan the front and back covers, inside flaps, the foreword, introduction, table of contents, chapter headings, pictures and graphs. What's your impression of the book? What stands out? What are your expectations?

Remember, asking yourself questions as you superscan will increase your comprehension. When you're ready, move on to the first chapter and scan for important ideas and topic sentences that will provide a preview of the material. Use the gold medal page-turning technique to keep your momentum and concentration high. When you're finished, begin a Mind Map of your thoughts and the key ideas from the section.

5. Read

This is where all your work pays off. Return to the material you just superscanned. If you lose focus, stop immediately and return to step two to get back into alpha state. Use your eye and hand skills. See groups of words, and use a visual guide. Push yourself ahead. At first you may want to stick with line-by-line reading. But as your speed builds, you can use the halfpipe or ski method to increase your reading speed. Underline or highlight key ideas, adding to your Mind Map as you go. You will use these notes to complete your reading upgrade in the next, and final, step of the quantum reader system.

Chapter 6: Review

Save Now, Succeed Later

Your upgrade is 90% complete

Have you ever lost important data because you were working too fast and forgot to save it? Be sure to back up all the information you read and save it in your brain with this final step in the quantum reader system: **Review**.

Mind Map. Tell back. You can say these words to yourself to remember how Mind Maps help you thoroughly digest and remember what you've read. Reread the underlined and highlighted sections. Next, complete your Mind Map. When you're finished, you can even turn the Mind Map over and try to recreate it from memory. Include new information and connections as they pop into your mind. Keep your Mind Map folded in the front of your book. You can read it whenever you need a quick review of the main ideas in the book.

Another great way to improve your comprehension is to share what you learned with someone else. Sharing your ideas will encourage others to do the same. It's an upward spiral of learning that you can ride to the top.

Using the quantum reader system always increases your speed and comprehension so you can learn more, have more fun, and have time left over to do more things that interest you. When you use the system, you can think about it like a big eagle that hovers, circles, swoops, pounces, devours and digests its target!

3. USE EYE AND HAND SKILLS

2. GET INTO STATE

1. PREPARE

4. SUPERSCAN

6. REVIEW   **5. READ**

Picture that eagle high in the sky circling, as you **PREPARE** and **GET INTO STATE**. Remember to **USE EYE AND HAND SKILLS** as you get ready to read. See the eagle swoop down closer and closer, getting ready to pounce, just like you're doing when you **SUPER-SCAN** the material to pique your curiosity and interest. Then, *pow*: The eagle pounces on its target and you pounce on your target and begin to **READ**, devouring your material with speed and interest. And like the eagle digesting its prey, you **REVIEW** what you've read

43

and savor what you've learned with Mind Maps, sharing and highlighted notes.

Picture the eagle as you practice the quantum reader system. After you've read your material, you'll notice the difference immediately. In fact, let's check your increased speed and comprehension right now.

To check your increased speed, return to *The Einstein Factor* and continue reading where you left off. Time yourself for one minute. When you're finished reading and answering the corresponding questions, return to page 3 to calculate your increased speed and comprehension.

Remember, genius comes from upgrading your life through learning to follow your interests, curiosity and passions.

Your upgrade is 100% complete

Use your reading power to discover and share the awe and wonder in your world.

Congratulations!
You're a Quantum Reader

Now you have a powerful six-step reading system to read faster, comprehend more and find the ideas that will spark your potential. Reading more effectively helps you keep up with your curiosity and learn more about the things that matter to you. Put your new reading skills to work to follow your interests, discover your passions, and find answers right away instead of letting ideas slip away.

In today's quantum world, you need fast skills and vast knowledge to learn more, be more and do more. Use your reading upgrade to share and expand your ideas and get the results you want out of school and life.

The Einstein Factor

by Win Wenger, Ph.D., and Richard Poe

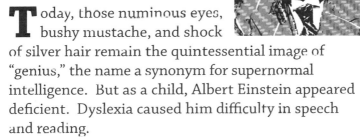

Today, those numinous eyes, bushy mustache, and shock of silver hair remain the quintessential image of "genius," the name a synonym for supernormal

5 intelligence. But as a child, Albert Einstein appeared deficient. Dyslexia caused him difficulty in speech and reading.

"Normal childhood development proceeded slowly," recalled his sister. "He had such difficulty with language

10 that they feared that he would never learn to speak... Every sentence he uttered, he repeated to himself, softly, moving his lips. This habit persisted into his seventh year."

Later, poor language skills provoked his Greek

15 teacher to tell the boy, "you will never amount to anything." Einstein was expelled from high school. He flunked a college entrance exam. After finally completing his bachelor's degree, he failed to attain a recommendation from his professors and was forced

20 to take a lowly job in a Swiss patent office. Until his mid-20s, he seemed destined for a life of mediocrity. Yet when he was 26, Einstein published his Special Theory of Relativity. Sixteen years later, he won a Nobel prize.

25   What did Einstein have that we don't? That's what Dr. Thomas Harvey wanted to know. He was the pathologist on duty at Princeton Hospital when Einstein died in 1955. By sheer chance, fate had fingered Harvey to perform Einstein's autopsy.

30 Without permission from the family, Harvey took it upon himself to remove and keep Einstein's famous brain. For the next 40 years, Harvey stored the brain in jars of formaldehyde, studying it slice by slice under the microscope and dispersing small samples to other

35 researchers on request.

    "Nobody had ever found a difference that earmarked a brain as that of a genius," Harvey later explained to a reporter. Neither he nor his colleagues found any definitive sign that would mark Einstein's brain as

40 extraordinary according to the ideas of brain physiology of that time. But in the early 1980s, Marian Diamond, a neuroanatomist at the University of California at Berkeley, made some discoveries about brains in general and Einstein's in particular that could revolutionize

45 ideas about genius and help entrepreneurs who want to become more innovative.

    One of Diamond's experiments was with rats. One group she placed in a super-stimulating environment with swings, ladders, treadmills, and toys. The

50 other group was confined to bare cages. The rats in the big-stimulus environment not only lived to the advanced age of 3 (the equivalent of 90 in a man), but their brains increased in size, sprouting new glial cells, which make connections between neurons (nerve

55 cells). As long ago as 1911, Santiago Ramón y Cajal,

father of neuroanatomy, had found that the number of interconnects between neurons was a far better predictor of brain power than the sheer number of neurons.

60   So, in rats, Diamond had created the physical footprint of higher intelligence through mental exercise. She then examined sections of Einstein's brain – and found that it, too, was unusually "interconnected." It had a larger-than-normal number
65 of glial cells in the left parietal lobe, which is a kind of neurological switching station that connects the various areas of the brain. It has long been known that unlike neurons, which do not reproduce after we are born, the connective hardware of the brain – glial
70 cells, axons, and dendrites – can increase in number throughout life, depending on how you use your brain. The more we learn, the more of these pathways are created. When we learn a skill such as riding a bicycle, we create connections between brain cells that remain
75 for decades. Mental power is, in a way, connective power.

A "Retarded" Achievement

       Was Einstein's mental development affected by some analogy to the swings, ladders, treadmills, and
80 toys of Diamond's super-rats? Did he, in some sense, learn his inventive mental powers? Einstein himself seemed to think so. He believed that you could stimulate ingenious thought by allowing the imagination to float freely, forming associations at will. For instance,

85 he attributed his Theory of Relativity not to any special
    gift, but to what he called his "retarded" development.
        "A normal adult never stops to think about
    problems of space and time," he said. These are things
    which he has thought of as a child. But my intellectual
90 development was retarded, and I began to wonder
    about space and time only when I had already
    grown up."
        In his *Autobiographical Notes*, Einstein recalled
    having the first crucial insight that led to his Special
95 Theory of Relativity at age 16 while he was daydreaming.
        As a boy, Einstein had a favorite uncle named
    Jakob who used to teach him mathematics. "Algebra is
    a merry science," said Jakob once. "We go hunting for
    a little animal whose name we don't know, so we call
100 it x. When we bag our game, we pounce on it and give
    it its right name." Uncle Jakob's words stayed with
    Einstein for the rest of his life. They encapsulated his
    attitude toward mathematical and scientific problems,
    which to Einstein always seemed more like puzzles or
105 games than work. Einstein could focus on his math
    studies with the concentration most children reserve
    for play.
        "What would it be like," Einstein wondered, "to
    run beside a light beam at the speed of light?" Normal
110 adults would squelch such a question and forget it.
    Einstein was different. He played with this question
    for 10 years. The more he pondered, the more
    questions arose. Suppose, he asked himself, that you
    were riding on the end of a light beam and held a
115 mirror before your face. Would you see your reflection?

According to classical physics, you would not – because light leaving your face would have to travel faster than light in order to reach the mirror. But Einstein could not accept this. It didn't feel right. It seemed ludicrous that you would look into a mirror and see nothing. Einstein imagined rules for a universe that would allow you to see your reflection in a mirror while riding a light beam. Only years later did he undertake proving his theory mathematically.

Einstein attributed his scientific prowess to what he called "vague play" with "sign," "images," and other elements, both "visual" and "muscular." "This comminatory play," he wrote, "seems to be the essential feature in productive thought."

My project of the last 25 years had been to develop techniques and mental exercises, based in part on Einstein's methods, that work in the short term and also develop the mind's permanent powers.

Einstein is the most spectacular modern example of a man who could dream while wide awake. With few exceptions, the great discoveries in science were made through such intuitive "thought experiments."

Inventor Elias Howe labored long and hard to create the first sewing machine. Nothing worked. One night, Howe had a nightmare. He was running from a band of cannibals – they were so close, he could see their spear tips. Despite his terror, Howe noticed each spear point had a hole bored in its tip like the eye of a sewing needle.

When he awoke, Howe realized what his nightmare was trying to say: On his sewing machine, he needed to move the eyehole from the middle of the needle down to the tip. That was his breakthrough, and the sewing machine was born.

150   Insights from dreams have inspired rulers, artists, scientists, and inventors since Biblical times. But day after day, year after year, the vast majority of people squelch their most profound insights without even knowing it. This defensive reflex – which I call The

155 Squelcher – blocks us from achieving our full potential.

But dreams have their limitations. They are notoriously hard to control. We have not yet learned how to summon them at will. And, most of the time, we forget them.

160   In March 1977, a group of us had heard about the revolutionary experiments Russian scientists were making by tapping the subconscious for accelerated learning. Although no one at that time had published reliable accounts of the exact proce-

165 dures, we reconstructed these as best we could from odd corners of the scientific literature. We decided to conduct an experiment in a friend's apartment in Arlington, Virginia.

We were completely surprised. Nearly every tech-

170 nique produced striking results for almost everyone in the group. Especially memorable was the experience of a participant who I shall call "Mary." Like all of us, she had agreed to embark upon some new learning experiment just prior to the workshop. She chose the violin.

175 Mary had her first lesson just one week before our experiment. Until that time, she had never touched a violin in her life.

The week following our workshop, Mary had her second lesson. She worked as a secretary in a Washington office and had only a moderate amount of time to practice. Nevertheless, after Mary had played a few minutes, her astonished instructor announced that he was going to reenroll her in his advanced class! At our second experimental workshop, just a few weeks later, Mary gave a fine concert with her violin.

Mary owed her precocious ability to the "Raikov Effect." Using deep hypnosis, Soviet psychiatrist Dr. Vladimir Raikov made people think that they had become some great genius in history. When he "reincarnated" someone as Rembrandt, the person could draw with great facility. Later, the subject remembered nothing. Many would scoff in disbelief when shown artwork they had drawn under hypnosis.

Raikov demonstrated that talents unleashed under hypnosis left significant effects even after the sessions. So the method was more than an experimental oddity. It was a practical tool for learning. Moreover, as we were to discover it could be achieved without the aid of hypnosis.

Note the number of lines you read and multiply it by 8. This is your current reading speed.

If you would like to read more, this excerpt was taken from *The Einstein Factor* (Prima Publishing, Rocklin, California, 1995)

55

Reading Comprehension Test
The Einstein Factor

(TRUE or FALSE. Questions 1-10 apply to lines 1-95. Questions 11-20 apply to lines 96-199.)

1. Einstein suffered from dyslexia.   **T F**

2. Einstein was expelled from college.   **T F**

3. Einstein published the Theory of Relativity   **T F**
when he was 26.

4. Einstein died in 1955.   **T F**

5. Einstein's brain was stored in a jar for 50   **T F**
years.

6. Marian Diamond was a neuroanatomist at   **T F**
the University of California at San Diego.

7. Marian Diamond's experiments on rats   **T F**
increased the size of the rats' brains.

8. Santiago Ramón y Cajal is the father of   **T F**
neuroanatomy.

9. Einstein believed he had retarded   **T F**
development.

10. Einstein was asleep and dreaming when he   **T F**
discovered the Theory of Relativity.

11. Einstein practiced trigonometry while   **T F**
hunting with his uncle.

12. Einstein used to wonder what it would be   **T F**
like to run beside a beam of light.

13. According to classical physics, if you were   **T F**
riding a the end of a beam of light with a
mirror held in front of your face, you
would see your reflection.

14. Einstein attributed his scientific prowess to "vague play." **T F**

15. Einstein could dream while he was awake. **T F**

16. The inventor Elias Howe created the first sewing machine during a dream about cannibals. **T F**

17. Russian scientists conducted experiments on the subconscious for accelerated learning. **T F**

18. Mary was a secretary in Washington. **T F**

19. The Raikov Effect made people think they were dreaming. **T F**

20. The Raikov Effect left no effects afterwards. **T F**

Answers:
1. T
2. F
3. T
4. T
5. F
6. F
7. T
8. T
9. T
10. F
11. F
12. T
13. F
14. T
15. T
16. T
17. T
18. T
19. F
20. F

About the Author

Bobbi DePorter

Bobbi DePorter is the cofounder of SuperCamp and president of Quantum Learning Network (QLN). Based in Oceanside, California, QLN is a global education leader impacting more than 2 million youth and adults from 50 states and 80 countries with programs for personal and academic excellence. Her previous books include *Quantum Success*, *Quantum Teaching*, *Quantum Learning* and *The Seven Biggest Teen Problems And How To Turn Them Into Strengths,* and have been printed in seven languages with worldwide distribution.

Books by Bobbi DePorter

The Quantum Upgrade Series
Quantum Learner
Quantum Reader
Quantum Writer
Quantum Memorizer
Quantum Thinker
Quantum Note-Taker

Quantum Success: 8 Key Catalysts to Shift Your Energy into Dynamic Focus
Quantum Business: Achieving Success through Quantum Learning
Quantum Teaching: Orchestrating Student Success
Quantum Learning: Unleashing the Genius in You
The 8 Keys of Excellence: Principles to Live By
The Seven Biggest Teen Problems And How To Turn Them Into Strengths

How to Contact the Quantum Learning Network

By Phone: (760) 722-0072
By Mail: Quantum Learning Network
      1938 Avenida del Oro
      Oceanside, CA 92056

Online: www.QLN.com

Receive your complimentary *"I am a Quantum Learner"* poster at www.QuantumLearner.com.

International associate offices in Taiwan, China, Hong Kong, South Korea, Malaysia, Singapore, Indonesia, Mexico, Dominican Republic and Switzerland